MULTIFAMILY MASTERY

Unlocking Financial Freedom Through
Real Estate Investing

By Supercrown Vault

Table of Contents

3

CHAPTER 1

INTRODUCTION

Welcome to "Multifamily Mastery," a comprehensive resource designed to guide you through the intricate world of investing in multifamily properties. This book is crafted for investors at all levels, whether you're making your first foray into real estate investment or you're an experienced investor looking to expand your portfolio with multifamily assets.

Our goal is to provide you with the knowledge, strategies, and insights necessary to navigate the multifamily real estate market with confidence and success.

Multifamily real estate, encompassing properties with two or more residential units, presents a unique and lucrative opportunity for investors. From duplexes and triplexes to large apartment complexes, multifamily properties offer the potential for significant financial rewards, including steady cash flow, capital appreciation, and tax benefits.

However, like all investments, they come with their own set of challenges and risks. Understanding these nuances is key to making informed decisions that align with your financial goals.

This eBook is structured to take you step by step through the entire process of multifamily real estate investing. We'll start with the basics, introducing you to the concept of multifamily investment and why it stands out in the real estate market.

You'll learn about the different types of multifamily properties, how to analyze and select the right investment opportunities, and the financial considerations unique to these types of investments.

We'll dive deep into the strategies for acquiring and financing multifamily properties, including traditional loans, government-backed financing, and creative financing options. You'll gain insights into conducting due diligence, evaluating property potential, and understanding market dynamics to ensure your investment decisions are sound and profitable.

Furthermore, this guide will cover the critical aspects of property management, from tenant selection and retention to maintenance and renovations, ensuring your investment continues to grow in value over time.

We'll also explore the legal and regulatory landscape affecting multifamily properties, helping you navigate the complexities of leases, zoning laws, and compliance issues.

Throughout this guide, we'll share real-world examples, case studies, and expert tips to illustrate key points and strategies. These practical insights will equip you with the tools and confidence needed to succeed in the multifamily real estate market.

Whether you're looking to generate passive income, build wealth, or diversify your investment portfolio, "The Complete Guide To Multifamily Real Estate Investing" is an indispensable resource.

Let's embark on this exciting journey together, unlocking the doors to financial freedom and success in multifamily real estate investing.

CHAPTER 2

MULTIFAMILY PROPERTY OVERVIEW

This chapter is all about giving you a solid foundation on multifamily properties, covering everything from the basics to more specialized topics. Let's break it down into easy-to-understand sections.

The 3 Main Types of Multifamily Properties

1. Small Multifamily Properties: These include duplexes (two units), triplexes (three units), and fourplexes (four units). They're a great starting point for new investors because they can be easier to manage and finance, almost like buying a single-family home but with the bonus of extra rental income.

2. Mid-sized Multifamily Properties: These are buildings with roughly five to 50 units. They require a bit more management and offer more income potential. It's a step up for investors ready to handle more tenants and possibly hire a property manager.

3. Large Multifamily Properties: Think apartment complexes with 50+ units. Investing in these is a significant leap, often involving professional property management teams, larger investment capital, and a deeper understanding of the real estate market.

Property Classes

Properties are also categorized into classes based on their condition, location, and amenities:

Class A: Newest buildings with top amenities in prime locations. High rent, but costly to buy.

Class B: Slightly older buildings, still in good areas. A balance of reasonable rents and investment cost.

Class C: Older buildings, possibly needing some work, in less desirable areas. They offer higher cash flow potential due to lower acquisition costs.

Specialized Multifamily Housing

Student Housing: Located near colleges or universities, these properties cater to students. They can offer high demand but also come with seasonal turnover and unique management challenges.

Senior Housing: Designed for older adults, these can range from independent living to assisted living facilities. They're growing in demand as the population ages.

Affordable Housing & LIHTC (Low-Income Housing Tax Credit): These properties offer reduced rents to lower-income tenants, supported by government programs. Investors can benefit from tax credits but must navigate regulatory requirements.

Multifamily Value Drivers
The value of multifamily properties can be driven by various factors:

Location: Proximity to amenities, employment centers, and good schools.
Occupancy Rates: High occupancy means steady income.
Rental Income: The amount of income the property generates.

Operational Efficiency: Managing expenses to maximize profits.

Market Fluctuations: Economic downturns can affect occupancy and rent.
Management Challenges: Dealing with tenants and maintenance can be
time-consuming.

Financial Risks: High leverage or unexpected expenses can impact
profitability.

Rent vs. Buy Analysis Exercise

Understanding whether to rent out your property or consider selling it
depends on market conditions, your financial goals, and the property's
performance. Analyzing cash flow, appreciation potential, and your
investment strategy is crucial.

Multifamily Opportunities: In-Depth Examples

Example 1: Small Multifamily Flip
Imagine buying a triplex in need of minor renovations. By updating the units
and improving management, you can increase rents, thus raising the
property's value. After a year or two, you might sell it for a significant profit.

Example 2: Large Multifamily Value-Add
Consider a 100-unit apartment complex that's been neglected. With a
strategic investment in renovations and marketing, you can enhance its
appeal, boost occupancy, and increase rental income, substantially growing
its value over time.

Multifamily properties offer a range of investment opportunities, from
hands-on projects to more passive income strategies. Understanding the
types of properties, how to classify them, and the unique aspects of
specialized housing can help you find the right investment.

Keep in mind tho value drivers and risks as you conduct your rent vs. buy analysis. By diving into real-world examples, you can better visualize the potential and challenges of multifamily investing.

CHAPTER 3

MULTIFAMILY EXPENSE DRIVERS

After diving into how to boost your property's income, it's time to tackle the other side of the equation: expenses. Managing your multi family property's expenses wisely is just as important as maximizing revenue. Think of your property like a boat; income is the wind in your sails, but unchecked expenses are leaks that can slow you down or even sink you.

Let's patch up those leaks by understanding the main expense drivers in multifamily investing.

Property Taxes

Property taxes are like a membership fee for the privilege of owning property in a certain area. They're based on the assessed value of your property and can vary widely by location. High property taxes can eat into your profits, so it's important to factor them into your budget. For example, if your property is assessed at $500,000 and the local property tax rate is 2%, you're looking at $10,000 per year in property taxes.

Insurance

Insurance is your safety net, protecting your investment from unforeseen disasters like fires, floods, or lawsuits. The cost depends on the coverage amount, the type of property, and the level of risk.

A 20-unit building might have an annual insurance premium of $5,000 for basic coverage. It's a necessary expense to safeguard your investment.

Repairs & Maintenance

Keeping your property in tip-top shape is crucial for tenant satisfaction and property value. Repairs and maintenance can include everything from fixing leaky faucets to painting and landscaping. Think of it as routine healthcare for your property. Allocating 1-2% of your property's value annually for maintenance—say $5,000 for a $500,000 property—is a good rule of thumb.

Personnel Costs

If your property is large enough to require onsite staff, personnel costs become a significant expense. This includes salaries for property managers, maintenance staff, and leasing agents. For a mid-sized property, you might spend $30,000 a year on personnel costs.

Efficient management can help control these expenses while maintaining high service levels.

General & Administrative (G&A) and Marketing Costs

G&A covers the daily running costs of your property, like office supplies and utility bills for common areas. Marketing costs are what you spend to attract new tenants, such as online listings or signage. Together, these could amount to several thousand dollars a year, depending on your property's size and market competition.

Property Management Fees

If you hire an external company to manage your property, you'll pay property management fees. These are usually a percentage of the gross rental income, often between 8% and 12%. For a property generating $20,000 in monthly rent, a 10% management fee would be $2,000 per month. It's a significant expense, but professional management can enhance your property's value and operational efficiency.

Capital Expense Reserves

Think of capital expense reserves as a savings account for big future expenses—replacing the roof, upgrading the HVAC system, or renovating units to keep them competitive. Setting aside a portion of your income regularly can prevent these large expenses from becoming financial burdens. A common practice is to reserve about $250 to $400 per unit per year, depending on the property's age and condition.

Real-World Example

Let's consider a 20-unit property with a GPR of $240,000 annually ($1,000 per unit per month). Here's how expenses might break down in a year:

- Property Taxes**: $10,000
- Insurance**: $5,000
- Repairs & Maintenance**: $10,000 (assuming 2% of property value)
- Personnel Costs**: $30,000 (for onsite management and maintenance staff)
- G&A and Marketing Costs**: $5,000
- Property Management Fees**: $24,000 (10% of gross rental income)
- Capital Expense Reserves**: $8,000 ($400 per unit)

Total annual expenses: $92,000

Understanding and managing these expenses is crucial. They directly impact your property's net operating income (NOI) and, by extension, its value. By strategically managing each expense category, you can enhance your property's profitability and long-term growth potential.

CHAPTER 4

MULTIFAMILY DEBT FINANCING

When it comes to growing your multifamily real estate portfolio, understanding how to navigate the world of debt financing is like learning to sail in open water. It's all about leveraging loans to fuel your investments without getting caught in a storm.

This chapter will guide you through the essentials of multifamily debt financing, from sourcing the loan to understanding the fine print that comes with it.

Sourcing the Loan

Finding the right loan for your multifamily property is like searching for the perfect crew for your ship. You want partners who understand your goals and can navigate you to success.

This journey often starts with commercial banks, credit unions, or mortgage brokers specializing in real estate financing. Each lender offers different terms, so it's important to shop around and find the best fit for your project.

Loan Terms

Loan terms are the rules of the voyage. They detail how long you have to pay back the loan (typically 5 to 30 years for multifamily properties) and the interest rate.

Some loans have fixed rates, locking in your costs for the loan's life, while others have adjustable rates, which can change based on market conditions.

Amortization vs. Term

Amortization is the schedule by which you'll pay off the loan, often stretching beyond the loan's term. For example, a loan might have a 30-year amortization but a 10-year term, meaning you'll have payments as if the loan lasts 30 years, but you'll need to refinance or pay off the remaining balance after 10 years. This setup can offer lower monthly payments but requires planning for the loan's future.

Interest-Only Periods

Some loans offer an interest-only period, during which you only pay the interest on the loan, not the principal. This can be helpful for improving cash flow in the early years of your investment. Imagine it as having a lighter load to carry as you start your journey, allowing you to allocate funds elsewhere, like renovations or other investments.

Future Funding

Future funding, or loan advances, are provisions in a loan that allow you to borrow more money in the future for property improvements or expansions. It's like having a reserve tank you can tap into when you want to boost your property's value or income potential.

Prepayment Penalties

Prepayment penalties are fees charged by lenders if you pay off your loan early. Lenders include these clauses to ensure they make a profit on the loan, even if you find a way to settle it sooner than expected. It's crucial to understand these penalties as they can significantly impact your exit strategy and overall investment costs.

Loan Sizing

Loan sizing is determining how much you can borrow based on the property's value and income. Lenders use metrics like the Loan to Value (LTV) ratio and Debt Service Coverage Ratio (DSCR) to assess risk and decide on the loan amount. It's a balance between what you think the property needs and what the lender deems safe.

Loan Covenants

Loan covenants are the promises you make to the lender, including how you'll operate the property and financial benchmarks you must maintain. Violating these covenants can lead to default, even if you're making all your payments. Think of them as the map you agree to follow throughout your loan's life.

Real-World Example

Let's say you're financing a $2 million multifamily property. You secure a loan with a 75% LTV, meaning you borrow $1.5 million. The loan has a 10-year term with a 30-year amortization and an initial 5-year interest-only period. Your interest rate is 4%.

For the first 5 years, you pay interest only, which lowers your monthly payment and improves your cash flow, allowing you to reinvest in the property or other projects. However, you must plan for higher payments once the interest-only period ends and you begin paying down the principal.

Understanding these financing elements helps you better navigate the multifamily real estate investment seas, making informed decisions to grow your portfolio while managing risks.

CHAPTER 5

MULTIFAMILY UNDERWRITING PROCESS

This section is how lenders and investors evaluate the financial health and potential of a property before making a lending or investment decision. Let's dive into the key components of the multifamily underwriting process: the Offering Memorandum (OM), the rent roll & T-12, and commercial leases.

The Offering Memorandum (OM)

The Offering Memorandum (OM) is like the treasure map of real estate investing. It's a detailed document provided by the seller or broker that gives you a comprehensive overview of the property. The OM includes information such as property descriptions, financial data, market analysis, and projections.

Think of it as the brochure that highlights all the reasons why this property is worth your investment. For example, an OM might showcase a 100-unit apartment complex's amenities, occupancy rates, and income potential, aiming to persuade investors of its value.

The Rent Roll

The rent roll is the ledger of your voyage, listing all the tenants, their lease terms, and how much rent they pay. It's a snapshot of the property's current income, and by analyzing it, you can gauge the stability and financial health of the investment.

For instance, a rent roll will show you if most tenants are on long-term leases or if there's a high turnover, which could signal potential issues or opportunities for rent increases.

T-12 (Trailing 12 Months)

The T-12, or trailing 12 months financial statement, is the logbook of the property's financial performance over the past year. It includes detailed income and expense reports, offering a clear picture of the property's operational efficiency.

Analyzing the T-12 helps you understand where the money is coming from and going to, identifying areas for improvement or confirming the property's profitability. For example, a T-12 might reveal that utility costs are unusually high, indicating an opportunity for cost-saving measures.

Commercial Leases

Understanding commercial leases is crucial in multifamily investing. These documents outline the terms agreed upon by the landlord (you) and the tenants, including rent amounts, lease durations, and responsibilities for repairs and maintenance.

Commercial leases can vary widely, and their terms significantly impact your investment's profitability and management. For example, a lease might include a clause that tenants are responsible for minor repairs, reducing your maintenance expenses.

Real-World Example

Let's consider you're interested in purchasing a multifamily property listed at $5 million. You receive the OM, which highlights the property's modern amenities, 95% occupancy rate, and annual income potential of $600,000. The rent roll shows a healthy mix of one-year and two-year leases, with an average rent of $1,500 per unit, suggesting stable income.

The T-12 indicates operating expenses of $200,000, leading to a net operating income (NOI) of $400,000. By examining commercial leases, you confirm that tenants are responsible for utilities, potentially lowering operating costs.

Armed with this information, you can assess the property's value, predict its cash flow, and decide on a fair offer. The underwriting process, with its detailed analysis and documentation, ensures you make an informed decision, minimizing risks and setting the stage for a successful investment.

Understanding the multifamily underwriting process is like having a compass on your investment journey. It guides you through the financial landscape of a property, helping you make decisions with confidence and precision. In the chapters ahead, we'll explore strategies for managing and optimizing your multifamily investment, ensuring your voyage is both profitable and smooth.

CHAPTER 6

MODELING THE DEAL

To reach your destination safely and profitably, you need a detailed map and a plan. In real estate investing, creating a "model" of your deal is your map and plan. This model helps you predict how the investment will perform, guiding your decisions and strategies.

Let's navigate through the essentials of modeling a multifamily real estate deal, focusing on the pro forma model, data inputs, assumptions, and more.

The Pro Forma Model

The pro forma model is like your treasure map, showing the expected income, expenses, and cash flow of the property over a certain period. It's a financial model that projects future financial performance based on certain assumptions.

For instance, it can show how much income you can expect if occupancy rates rise or how expenses might increase with inflation.

Data Inputs

Data inputs are the coordinates you plot on your map. They're the factual numbers and information you use to build your model, such as current rents, vacancy rates, operating expenses, and market growth rates.

For example, you might input the current average rent of $1,200 per unit and a 5% annual market rent increase into your model.

Modeling Assumptions

Assumptions are the winds that can change your course; they're your educated guesses about how factors affecting your investment will behave in the future. This can include expected vacancy rates, rent growth, expense inflation, and capital improvements costs.

For example, you might assume a 2% annual increase in operating expenses and a $500,000 cost for property upgrades over the next five years.

Capital & Debt Assumptions

Capital and debt assumptions are like calculating the size of your ship and the weight it can carry. These assumptions deal with the financial structure of your deal, including how much equity you'll invest, the terms of your mortgage, interest rates, and loan amortization.

For instance, you might assume a 75% loan-to-value (LTV) ratio for your mortgage, a 4% interest rate, and a 30-year amortization period.

Sale Assumptions

Sale assumptions forecast the end of your journey, predicting how and when you might sell the property and for how much. This includes estimating the property's future sale price based on its expected income at the time of sale and the market conditions.

You might assume you'll sell the property in 10 years at a 5% capitalization rate, based on its projected net operating income (NOI).

Real-World Example

Let's model a deal for a multifamily property you're considering purchasing for $2 million:

Data Inputs: The property has 20 units, with current rents averaging $1,200 per unit per month. The vacancy rate is 5%, and annual operating expenses are $80,000.

Modeling Assumptions: You assume rents will increase by 3% per year, operating expenses will rise by 2% annually, and you'll spend $200,000 on capital improvements in the next two years.

Capital & Debt Assumptions: You plan to put down 25% ($500,000) in equity and finance the rest with a loan at a 4% interest rate, with a 30-year amortization.

Sale Assumptions: You aim to sell the property in 10 years, projecting a 5% capitalization rate based on your estimated NOI at that time.

Using these inputs and assumptions, you build a pro forma model that projects your property's financial performance, helping you decide if this investment aligns with your goals. By adjusting the assumptions, you can see how changes might affect your investment's outcome, allowing you to plan for various scenarios.

Modeling the deal is an essential skill in multifamily real estate investing. It allows you to anticipate challenges, explore opportunities, and make informed decisions. With practice, you'll become adept at navigating the financial seas, steering your investments toward success and profitability.

MULTIFAMILY DEAL ANALYSIS & VALUATION

Understanding how to analyze and value potential investments is like being able to read the stars in the sky – it guides you towards making informed decisions.

This chapter will illuminate the concepts of the Capitalization (Cap) rate, Internal Rate of Return (IRR), equity multiple, cash-on-cash return, and more, helping you navigate the complex world of multifamily valuation.

The Capitalization (Cap) Rate

The Cap rate is like the compass of real estate investing. It helps you determine the potential return on an investment, independent of financing. You calculate it by dividing the Net Operating Income (NOI) by the property's purchase price. For example, if a property's NOI is $100,000 and it's for sale at $1,000,000, the Cap rate would be 10%. A higher Cap rate suggests a potentially higher return, but often with higher risk.

The Internal Rate of Return (IRR)

The IRR is like calculating the speed of your ship over its entire journey, considering all inflows and outflows of cash, including the purchase, operational income, and sale of the property. It's a comprehensive way to evaluate an investment's profitability over time.

For instance, if your IRR is 15%, it means you're expected to average a 15% return annually on the money invested in the property over the investment period.

The Equity Multiple

Think of the equity multiple as the total distance traveled on your investment voyage. It shows how much money you'll make in total from your investment compared to your initial investment.

If you invest $100,000 and end up with $200,000 after selling the property, your equity multiple is 2x. This means you've doubled your investment.

The Cash-on-Cash Return

The cash-on-cash return is like checking how far your ship has sailed in a year, focusing solely on the cash income. It's calculated by dividing the annual pre-tax cash flow by the total cash invested.

If you invest $100,000 and receive $10,000 in cash flow a year, your cash-on-cash return is 10%. This measure is crucial for investors prioritizing current income.

Multifamily Valuation

Valuing a multifamily property is akin to estimating the worth of a treasure chest based on its contents. It involves using the Cap rate to determine the property's value based on its NOI.

If a similar property in your area sold with a Cap rate of 8% and your property's NOI is $80,000, then your property's estimated value would be $1,000,000 ($80,000 / 0.08).

What Are "Good" Returns?

Determining "good" returns is like setting your personal navigation stars. It depends on your investment goals, risk tolerance, and the market. Generally, a higher return suggests a better investment, but it often comes with higher risk.

"Good" returns are those that meet or exceed your targets given the risk you're willing to take.

Capital Risk Buckets

Capital risk buckets help you categorize investments based on their risk and return profile. Think of them as different routes you can take on the sea:

Core: Low risk, stable returns. Like sailing near the coast, it's safer but with modest returns.

Core-Plus: Slightly higher risk, with some value-add potential. Venturing a bit further into open waters for potentially better returns.

Value-Add: Medium to high risk, requiring operational or physical improvements. It's like searching for hidden treasures with a map.

Opportunistic: High risk, high return. Setting sail into the unknown, with the potential for great rewards.

Capital Risk Bucket Examples

For example, a "core" investment might be a fully leased, newly built apartment complex in a prime location with a Cap rate of 5%. A "value-add" investment could be an older complex with below-market rents and room for renovations, offering a Cap rate of 8%.

An "opportunistic" investment might involve developing a new complex in an unproven area, with projected IRRs above 20%.

Conclusion

Navigating through multifamily deal analysis and valuation requires a keen understanding of various financial metrics and how they relate to your investment goals.

By mastering these concepts, you can better assess the potential risks and rewards of each opportunity, guiding your investment strategy towards success.

As you continue your journey in multifamily investing, remember that each deal is a new voyage. With the knowledge you've gained, you're well-equipped to chart your course through the exciting and rewarding world of real estate investment.

UNDERWRITING THE DEAL

This chapter, "Underwriting the Deal," serves as your compass, guiding you through understanding multifamily markets, analyzing your competitive set, dissecting the unit mix, identifying other income drivers, and calculating the return on cost.

Understanding Multifamily Markets

Imagine a multifamily market as a vast ocean with different currents and weather patterns. Just as sailors must understand these conditions before setting sail, investors must grasp the economic, demographic, and real estate trends of their target market.

Look for growing job markets, stable or increasing population trends, and areas with high rental demand but limited supply. For example, a city with a burgeoning tech industry might attract a young workforce in need of housing, presenting a fertile ground for multifamily investments.

The Competitive Set

Knowing your competition is like understanding the other ships in the waters around you. The competitive set includes other multifamily properties in your target market that potential tenants might consider. Analyze these properties based on location, amenities, rent levels, occupancy rates, and tenant demographics.

This analysis helps you position your property effectively. For instance, if most competitors lack pet-friendly amenities and there's high demand for such features, offering them could give you a competitive edge.

The Unit Mix

The unit mix of a multifamily property is the assortment of apartment types it offers, such as studios, one-bedrooms, or two-bedrooms. It's like having a fleet with different types of ships, each serving a specific purpose. The right mix should align with the market demand in your area.

If your market analysis shows a high demand for one-bedroom apartments due to a significant number of single professionals, focusing on a property with a majority of one-bedroom units might be most profitable.

Other Income Drivers

Beyond rent, other income drivers can significantly impact your property's financial performance, similar to a ship having multiple sails to catch the wind. These can include fees for pet rent, parking, laundry facilities, and storage.

For example, in a high-demand urban area where parking is at a premium, charging for parking spaces could generate substantial additional income. Identifying and optimizing these income sources can enhance your property's overall revenue.

Return on Cost (ROC)

Return on Cost (ROC) is a metric that compares the property's expected income to its total cost (purchase price plus any renovation or development costs).

It's like measuring the efficiency of your ship in terms of speed versus the resources invested in it. A higher ROC indicates a more efficient use of capital. For instance, if you purchase a property for $1 million and spend another $500,000 on renovations, your total cost is $1.5 million. If the post-renovation annual NOI is $150,000, your ROC is 10%, a strong indicator of a good investment.

Real-World Example

Let's apply these concepts to a real-world scenario. Imagine you're considering purchasing a multifamily property in a mid-sized city with a growing healthcare industry.

Your market analysis reveals a demand for housing close to hospitals and clinics, primarily from medical professionals and support staff.

Competitive Set: Your analysis shows that nearby properties lack modern amenities and have high vacancy rates.

Unit Mix: You decide on a mix of one and two-bedroom units, catering to both single professionals and small families.

Other Income Drivers: Given the urban setting, you plan to offer premium parking and on-site fitness facilities for an additional fee.

Return on Cost: After calculating the expected income from rents and additional services against the purchase and renovation costs, you project an ROC that exceeds your target return, signaling a promising investment opportunity.

By thoroughly understanding each of these elements, you can underwrite multifamily deals with greater confidence and precision, steering your investments toward success in the competitive landscape of real estate.

As you continue your voyage in multifamily investing, remember that thorough preparation, in-depth analysis, and strategic execution are your best tools for navigating the complex and rewarding world of real estate investment.

CHAPTER 8

NAVIGATING TOWARDS SUCCESS

From understanding the basics of multifamily properties, diving deep into revenue and expense drivers, to mastering the art of deal analysis and valuation, this guide has equipped you with the knowledge and tools to navigate the lucrative yet challenging seas of real estate investment.

Final Thoughts

Multifamily real estate investing is not just about buying properties; it's about creating communities, understanding market dynamics, and making informed decisions that lead to financial growth and stability.

Remember, the key to successful investing is continuous learning, diligent analysis, and adapting to changing market conditions. Like any seasoned captain, an investor must be ready to adjust the sails when the wind changes direction.

Embrace the complexities of multifamily investing with patience and persistence. The challenges you face along the way are not obstacles but stepping stones to your success.

By applying the principles and strategies outlined in this book, you're well on your way to building a profitable and sustainable investment portfolio.

Good Cities for Multifamily Investment

As a parting gift, let's cast our eyes towards the horizon and explore some cities that show promising potential for multifamily investments. While market conditions can change, these cities have demonstrated strong growth indicators, including job creation, population growth, and rental demand.

1. Austin, Texas: With its booming tech industry and vibrant culture, Austin continues to attract young professionals and families, driving demand for rental properties.

2. Raleigh-Durham: North Carolina: Known for its Research Triangle Park, this area boasts a growing tech sector and a strong educational foundation, making it attractive for multifamily investments.

3. Nashville, Tennessee: A hub for the music industry and healthcare services, Nashville's diverse economy and cultural appeal make it a strong candidate for rental property investments.

4. Denver, Colorado: With its stunning natural scenery and robust job market, Denver has become a magnet for millennials, fueling the need for more multifamily housing options.

5. Orlando, Florida: Beyond its tourism appeal, Orlando's growing tech scene and no state income tax attract a steady stream of residents looking for multifamily living options.

Charting Your Course

As you set sail on your multifamily investing journey, keep in mind that every investor's path is unique. The cities mentioned above are just starting points.

Conduct thorough market research, stay informed about economic trends, and always perform comprehensive deal analysis to identify the best opportunities for your investment goals.

In closing, I hope this book serves as your compass in the vast ocean of multifamily investing, guiding you to prosperous shores. Remember, the journey of a thousand miles begins with a single step—or in our case, with a single property.

Here's to your success as a multifamily real estate investor. May your investments be fruitful, and your properties always be filled with happy tenants.

Happy investing!